THIS BOOK IS LOVINGLY PRESENTED TO:

_____

*As the mother of two daughters and the daughter of two mothers,
I dedicate this book to my birth mother who gave me life
and my adoptive mother who taught me how to live it.*

—Mary Ann

❧

To my mother, Madoline Ellison, and to my wife, Lesley.

—Chris

Text Copyright © 2009 Mary Ann McCabe Riehle
Illustration Copyright © 2009 Chris Ellison

Sleeping Bear Press™

310 North Main Street, Suite 300, Chelsea, MI 48118
www.sleepingbearpress.com

© 2009 Sleeping Bear Press is an imprint of Gale, a part of Cengage Learning.

Printed and bound in Canada.

10 9 8 7 6 5 4 3 2 1

Library of Congress Cataloging-in-Publication Data

Riehle, Mary Ann McCabe, 1959-
M is for mom : a child's alphabet / written by Mary Ann McCabe Riehle ;
Illustrated by Chris Ellison. -- 1st ed.
p. cm.
Summary: "Beginning with A and ending with Z, special moments and
interactions transpiring between mother and child are introduced with
poetry and prose. Topics include excitement, holding hands, questions,
stories, and wishes"--Provided by publisher.
ISBN 978-1-58536-458-9
1. Mother and child--Juvenile literature. 2. Mothers--Juvenile literature.
I. Ellison, Chris. II. Title.
HQ755.85.R434 2009
306.874'3--dc22
2009001395

M is for Mom

A Child's Alphabet

Written by Mary Ann McCabe Riehle
Illustrated by Chris Ellison

Hugs are important no matter how young or old you are and the hug between a mother and child is very special. Being held, hugged, and cuddled not only helps a baby bond with its mother and others but can also have a positive influence on the health and development of a baby. All of our five senses: sight, sound, smell, taste, and touch are important, but the sense of touch seems to be especially important to infants. Research has shown that babies who are held in their mother's arms for longer periods of time cry less and smile more. One study has also shown that premature babies who are held seem to gain weight faster and are able to go home from the hospital sooner.

"I love hugging. I wish I was an octopus, so I could hug ten people at a time."

—Drew Barrymore

A is for the Arms
that hug and hold me tight.
While in those arms I see your face
and know I'm in my favorite place.

A

Recipe for Mom's Special Treat:

Start with a little bit of extra sleep for Mom
Stir and wake gently
Mix in lots of hugs and kisses
Add a tray full of goodies
Enjoy!

Recipe for the caterpillar:

a leaf

"There is nothing in a caterpillar that tells
you it's going to be a butterfly."
—Richard Buckminster Fuller

Breakfast starts with letter B
and yummy things to eat.
Breakfast in bed
is a very special treat.

C is for the Critters
I collected in my jar.
You might think they're creepy
but I don't think they are.

Have you worn your mother's shoes and giggled at the clomp, clomp noise they make? If you wear Mom's party dress, does it make you feel like a princess? How about using your dad's tie as a belt? Or do you wear Daddy's button-down shirt and pretend you're going to work? Dressing up and putting on different outfits while dreaming of what it would be like to be a grown-up is fun.

"A grown-up is a child with layers on."

—Woody Harrelson

D is for Dress up
and looking grown-up too.
Looking in the mirror now
do I look more like you?

D E

E is for Excitement,
I can see it in your eyes
and I feel so good inside
when you're filled with pride.

Like birthstones and other symbols, each month of the year is represented by a different flower. What's your birth flower, your mom's, your grandma's?

January = carnation
February = violet
March = daffodil, jonquil
April = daisy, sweet pea
May = lily of the valley
June = rose
July = larkspur
August = gladiola
September = aster
October = calendula
November = chrysanthemum
December = poinsettia, narcissus

"A garden of love grows in a grandmother's heart."

—Author unknown

F is for the Flowers
that I picked for you.
I even found the ones
in your favorite color, too.

Grandma's garden for letter G
and picking flowers for all to see.
We'll put them in a special place
in Grandma's very special vase.

H Holding hands makes everything better,
so hand it to **H** for this letter.
When I hold your hand and you hold mine
I know that things will be just fine.

I is for "I love you,"
the words I love to hear
said quietly or loudly
or whispered in my ear.

J is for Juggling,
something that's very fun
unless you are trying
to get too many things done.

Our Kitchen is the room
that begins with letter K.
It's where we all gather
to begin our busy day.

Jugglers try to keep many things going at one time. Whether they are tossing balls, plates, or other objects in the air, they hope to catch them all and avoid a big mess. Have you ever seen your mom juggle? Juggling for a mom often means keeping everything on her busy schedule from spilling over. It's amazing how moms can juggle making dinner, helping with homework, volunteering, and working outside the home, yet still have time to toss in some fun with a kitchen full of kids!

J

K

Mother's Day is a special day to honor moms. In North America Mother's Day is celebrated on the second Sunday in May. Many countries throughout the world such as Denmark, Italy, Belgium, and Japan celebrate Mother's Day. In England the special day to honor mothers is called "Mothering Sunday."

Motherhood has been celebrated as far back in history as the ancient Greeks and Romans. In more recent history, the efforts of Anna Jarvis, also known as the Mother of Mother's Day, and Julia Ward Howe, the activist and writer, helped establish this official day to pay tribute to moms. The second Sunday in May was officially declared Mother's Day in the United States in 1914. In Canada the sale of greeting cards is at its highest for Mother's Day and it is one of the busiest days for phone calls.

"Mother love is the fuel that enables a normal human being to do the impossible."

—Marion C. Garretty

Letter L is for Lessons
and all I want to learn,
like how to ride my bike
and how to make it turn.

M is for Mother's Day,
a special day for you.
So I have a special gift—
I've learned to tie my shoes!

Name begins with letter N.
"Mom" is my name for you.
Momma, Mum, and Mommy
are other choices too.

Here is the word for "Mother" in a few other languages.
Arabic = Ahm
Bulgarian = Majka
Danish = Mor
French = Mère, Maman
Italian = Madre
Japanese = Okaasan, Haha
Yiddish = Muter

Children making early sounds in their native language are soon able to develop a name that gets a response from their mother. In North America the word "mother" and the variation of "momma" and its shortened form, "mom," come from Anglo-Saxon origins.

Some names for children are new and different and some are handed down from generation to generation. How was your name selected?

"When someone loves you, the way they say your name is different. You just know that your name is safe in their mouth."
—Author unknown, attributed to Billy, age 4

N
O

Once upon a time starts with an O,
my birth story begins,
it's my favorite, you know.

"Play is often talked about as if it were a relief from serious learning. But for children play is serious learning. Play is really the work of childhood."

Fred Rogers, host of *Mr. Rogers' Neighborhood,* who was known to wear sweaters knitted by his own mother.

"The noblest question in the world is 'What good may I do in it?'"

—Benjamin Franklin

P Q

Can we go to the Park today?
Please, please can we go and play?
And on the way to the playground can we see
how many things we find beginning with letter P?

Q is for the Questions
I'm always asking you.
Could you answer just one more?
Why is the sky so blue?

A bedtime story or reading a favorite book can be a great way to finish off a fun-filled day. Listening to a soothing song at the end of the day, or even at naptime, can help you relax. This kind of song is known as a lullaby. It is sung sweetly to quiet, calm, or lull a child to sleep. Do you have a favorite bedtime story or song?

Some famous lullabies:
"Hush, Little Baby"
"Lullaby and Good Night"
"Rock-a-Bye Baby"
"Twinkle, Twinkle Little Star "

"Reading is to the mind what exercise is to the body."

—Joseph Addison

R
S

R is for Reading, please
"Read it one more time."
It's my very favorite book.
I know every rhyme.

Letter S can be for Songs
shared at the end of the day.
But before you say good night,
could you switch on my little light?

T is for how Tall I am.
Not quite as tall as you.
        Measure me; I'm sure you'll see
        I've grown an inch or two.

                U is for Upside down
        and standing on my head.
                It's a different way to see things
        from down here instead.

T
U

Wishing on a star is something done in many cultures around the world. Why people wish on stars is not known for sure but it is an ancient practice. Stars were thought to have special powers and the first star in the evening may either have been thought to have more power or was just the first one seen and so it could be a faster way toward getting your wish granted. Try saying this poem the next time you see a star.

Star light, star bright,
First star I see tonight,
I wish I may, I wish I might,
Have the wish I wish tonight.

"Laughter is an instant vacation."

—Milton Berle

"A vacation is having nothing to do and all day to do it in."

—Robert Orben

V is for Vacation,
    a chance to stay up late
        or climb a tree and just feel free.
    Aren't vacations great?!

Wishing for letter W,
wanting your wish to really come true.
While W is a wonderful letter,
wishing on a star is even better.

The origins of Xs and Os representing kisses and hugs are not certain. Some believe the "X" represents pursed lips, puckered up for a kiss and the "O" is thought to represent the arms around someone in a hug.

Spending time on the sidelines is a fun way to share an activity and it's a good time for moms to use an "outside voice."

X Y

X is for lots of kisses
all lined up in a row,
with a hug here and there
if you add in an O.

Y for Yelling,
the good kind, not the bad.
When you're on the sidelines
that yelling makes me glad.

The alphabet ends with letter Z
but the fun is not done for you and me.
Can you guess what I want to do?
Let's please, please go to the Zoo!

Just because this book has come to the end doesn't mean the fun has to stop. Sometimes the ending of one thing is the beginning of another. Making memories is one of the best things moms and kids can do together, sharing special moments and milestones from A to Z and beyond.

"You'll be sort of surprised what there is to be found once you go beyond 'Z' and start poking around."

—Dr. Seuss

Z

Mary Ann McCabe Riehle

As a teacher, author, and mother, Mary Ann McCabe Riehle has motivated young students and adults to follow their dreams and tell their stories. A graduate of Xavier University with degrees in Communication Arts and Education, she has been a featured speaker at reading and writing conferences. She hopes that *M is for Mom*, her fourth children's book, will encourage readers, especially mothers and children, to remember and cherish special times together. Mary Ann lives in Dexter, Michigan, with her husband, Paul. She is also blessed and proud to be Bridget and Ellen's mom.

Chris Ellison

Chris Ellison received his formal art training at the Harris School of Art in Franklin, Tennessee, and then later at the Portfolio Center in Atlanta, Georgia. He has illustrated both children's picture books and adult historical fiction for the past 16 years. His first children's book, *King of the Stable*, was awarded the Gold Medallion from the Evangelical Christian Publishers Association in 1999. *M is for Mom* is Chris's fifth book for Sleeping Bear Press. His other titles include *The Lucky Star*, *Rudy Rides the Rails*, *Pappy's Handkerchief,* and his first book with Sleeping Bear Press, *Let Them Play,* was named a 2006 Notable Social Studies Trade Book for Young People. Chris lives in Petal, Mississippi, with his wife, Lesley, and two young sons.